THE
TENACIOUS DREAMS
OF
LISE MEITNER

Lise Meitner

Carolyn T. Reeves, Ed.D.

HENRY LYON BOOKS

FULTON, KY

Published by Henry Lyon Books
  an imprint of Master Design Publishing, LLC
  789 State Route 94 E, Fulton, KY 42041
  HenryLyonBooks.com

Cover design by Charli Kendricks and Rose Thomas.
Interior design by Faithe Thomas.

Photos/Images:
  Title Page, Chapters 1, 4, 5: Public Domain in the United States because it was published in the United States between 1926 and 1977, inclusive, without a copyright notice.
  Chapter 2: Public Domain, Courtesy Master and Fellows of Churchill College, Cambridge, England
  Chapter 3: Bundesarchiv, Bild 183-H1216-0500-002 / CC-BY-SA 3.0
  Chapter 6: © Deposit Photos, Charli Kendricks
  Chapter 7: Public Domain, Acc. 90-105 - Science Service, Records, 1920s-1970s, Smithsonian Institution Archives
  Chapter 8: This image is a work of a Nuclear Regulatory Commission employee, taken or made as part of that person's official duties. As a work of the U.S. federal government, the image is in the public domain in the United States.

Print ISBN: 978-1-947482-30-2
Ebook ISBN: 978-1-947482-32-6

Printed in the USA

TABLE OF CONTENTS

NOTE TO TEACHERS

The story of Lise Meitner dramatizes the changes that were unfolding around the world during the 1930s and 1940s. It allows students to evaluate critical issues such as women's rights, racism, discrimination, the origin of humans, differences in science and technology, plagiarism, the benefits of our American republic versus rule by dictators, the influence of Darwinian evolution on Hitler and other cultures, and the rise of Nazism.

This book can be added to any related science or history curriculum without disrupting the existing content. It will enrich students' knowledge about this important period of history and help them make connections that may not be obvious otherwise. Students should be encouraged to extend their knowledge of the events in this book.

Teacher discretion should determine whether to have students orally discuss the review questions or write their answers. Many of the questions are directly related to issues and problems in today's culture and are worth the time to explore.

PROLOGUE

Five hundred years before the first coming of Jesus, a young Jewish girl named Esther lost both of her parents during an attack on Israel by the Babylonian army. She was carried by force to the land of Babylon but was taken in and raised by her uncle. Soon afterward, the kingdom of Persia overtook Babylon. Then in a series of events ordained by God, Esther rose to the position of Queen of Persia and became an important part of exposing and thwarting an evil plan to kill all the Jews in the kingdom. This dramatic story is told in the biblical account of the book of Esther.

Twenty-five hundred years later, the German ruler, Adolph Hitler, devised an evil plan in which he plotted to completely eliminate all Jews from the face of the earth. Lise Meitner was conducting nuclear research in Berlin, Germany, as Hitler began to implement his plans. Like Esther before her, Lise found herself in the right place at the right time.

Lise's Jewish heritage made her a clear target. Forced to flee for her life to Sweden, Lise thought she had lost the opportunity to help find an explanation for the unexpected results from the nuclear research she and her coworkers were conducting. Because of her flight from Germany, she and her physicist nephew made an amazing discovery in Sweden about nuclear fission reactions, which was transferred to the American and Allied forces.

Many see God's hand in the defeat of Hitler and the Axis Powers as well as in the return of large numbers of surviving Jews to the land of their ancestors, known today as Israel.

CHAPTER 1

THE BIG DREAMS OF GISELA, GUSTI, AND LISE

The traditions of their Jewish neighborhood of Leopoldstadt rose up like invisible walls within the city of Vienna as the three Meitner sisters, ages 15, 14, and 13, contemplated their future. The Meitner girls were fully aware of the expectations of their Jewish ancestors, as well as the cultural and legal limits for the education and opportunities of young ladies of their day. Nevertheless, like their parents, they resisted many of these restraints and eagerly embraced the intellectual atmosphere that existed in their own home.

"Hey Gusti," Lise whispered trying to keep her mother from hearing them still talking after bedtime. "What do you plan to do after you graduate from school next week? Without waiting for an answer, she continued, "Lola is already engaged to be married."

"She won't be fifteen until July," Gusti sighed. "Getting married has been all Lola talked about for the past year. Elsie thinks she will be getting married next year too. Why can't we be like the boys and keep going to school? Everyone is wondering when I plan to get married now that I'm almost finished with school."

"Me too," Gisela said. Already 15, Gisela was the oldest child in the family and had finished the local public school last year. During the late 1800s, young ladies were not allowed to attend the universities of Austria, although occasionally a few were given permission to audit classes. "I think I would like to marry and have a family someday, but my dream is to attend medical school."

"Wow. That's some dream," Gusti remarked skeptically.

"What about you, Lise? Don't you want to get married some day?" Gusti asked.

"I'm not sure, but do you know what I really want to do?" Lise smiled knowing her dream was a long shot. "I want to be a real scientist someday, but I first want to attend the University for a long time and study math and science."

Gusti and Gisela giggled at Lise's outlandish dream, knowing that Lise often slept with her beloved math book under her pillow. At this time, most universities did not admit female students, especially in the fields of math and science.

Then Gusti spoke very softly. "I want be taught by the most accomplished musicians in Vienna and compose and write music. Then I want to play concerts."

This time Lise giggled, "And not get married?"

"There's no reason why I couldn't do both—be a professional musician and get married," Gusti retorted.

The next voice was her mother. "Don't you girls know it's too late to still be up talking? Get to sleep and talk tomorrow."

"Yes Ma'am," they said in unison, totally unaware that their unlikely dreams would come true for all of them, although they would be interrupted by an evil twist none of them could possibly have imagined. But that was decades away from their childhood dreams in the year 1892.

Review and Expand Your Knowledge

1. How were men and women treated differently during most of the nineteenth century in Austria when it came to opportunities to attend universities and acquire jobs? Were these problems also found in America?

2. Traditionally, what were young women in Austria expected to do within a few years after finishing public school?

CHAPTER 2

OVERCOMING THE OBSTACLES AND ACHIEVING THE DREAM

Most young women in Lise's home country of Austria ended their formal education at the age of fourteen and then married a few years later. But Lise had always wanted more. She was enamored with mathematics and the theoretical ideas of physics and dreamed of a career as a research scientist.

Those tenacious dreams overcame Lise's shy nature and the traditions of her era. The University of Vienna agreed to admit her as a student if she passed the rigorous entrance requirements, which she fully did. She persisted in completing the difficult work of getting a basic science degree.

A few women had ventured into fields of science and math, but many people still thought women shouldn't work in any scientific fields. There was an especially strong bias against women in the field of physics which was made up almost exclusively of males. It was her own father who understood her dreams and encouraged her to take on the challenge.

Despite the obstacles, Lise was admitted to the doctoral program where she achieved her goal of earning a doctorate in physics. In a decision typical of Lise, she still wanted to learn more, this time about quantum theory. She had recently met Dr. Planck at the University of Vienna where he took time in a private discussion with her to discuss his quantum theory. That meeting led her to move to Berlin, Germany, in order to study under Dr. Planck for a few semesters. But an unexpected opportunity opened a new door. She was invited to do research on radioactive elements at the Friedrich Wilhelm University as an assistant to Dr. Otto Hahn. The position was a perfect match for her dream job. However, it came with conditions most people would never have accepted. She would do her work as an unpaid "guest." As the only female scientist, she was not permitted to enter the chemistry labs with the male students. Her work with Otto was confined to a small basement room away from the rest of the Institute.

Nevertheless, this was the job she had dreamed of finding for years, and even with the negatives, she saw it as the best path for her future. During the first five years she lived in Berlin, she lived on a small allowance from her parents and parttime odd jobs.

In 1912, Otto and Lise moved their research to the new private Kaiser-Wilhelm Institute. Her life made a dramatic turn when she was informed that she would receive a title and a modest salary. As Assistant to Dr. Max Planck, she would grade his students' papers and still have time for her research with Otto. She was delighted to inform her parents she would no longer need their financial support.

When World War I began in 1914, Otto was called into military service. Lise signed up for x-ray technician training while continuing the research project she and Otto had begun. She volunteered as an x-ray technician with the Austrian army and also assisted in keeping operating tables and equipment cleaned and ready for use. Memories of the pain and suffering she saw during World War I would remain with her for the rest of her life.

By 1917, Lise had returned to Berlin to continue the Meitner-Hahn research. She wrote detailed letters to Otto of the results and kept him completely informed. Eventually the war ended, and conditions gradually returned to a more normal state. Throughout the war, Lise had managed to continue research on radioactive elements. Even during these difficult war years, she and Otto were able to publish important research.

Lise gradually overcame the misgivings her male coworkers had for a female scientist by demonstrating her exceptional abilities, intelligence, and talent. Although her salary remained small compared to male researchers, it gradually increased. She became an expected participant in international science conferences alongside Albert Einstein, Marie Curie, Neils Bohr, and other well-known scientists

As important as her work had become, her life in Berlin was not all about physics. Some of her favorite times were spent in the home of Max Planck for social gatherings and evenings of games and chamber music. Planck, an accomplished pianist, often performed musical pieces with his friend Albert Einstein who played the violin. Family members and other physicists with musical talent would showcase their talents. Even Otto sometimes joined in as a vocalist. Music was one of Lise's greatest pleasures. Most of her friends shared a common interest in physics, but a shared love for music and social outings cemented deep friendships with her fellow scientists and made her life even more satisfying than she could ever have imagined. She had fully achieved her dreams at last!. She considered her frugal lifestyle and the sacrifices she made during the early years in Berlin well worth the end results.

Review and Expand Your Knowledge

1. Find the meanings of these terms: *prejudice, bias, discrimination, propaganda, and racism*. Tell how Lise Meitner was affected by these problems.
2. During the time when Lise was attending universities and finding her first job, were young women encouraged to prepare for or begin a career in science? Is that still true today?
3. What unfair working conditions did Lise agree to when she first began conducting research in Berlin, Germany?
4. How did Lise overcome the misgivings her male coworkers had for women scientists?
5. Name several well-known people who were contemporaries of Lise.
6. Who was Dr. Otto Hahn?
7. Who was Dr. Max Planck?

CHAPTER 3

DREAMS COLLIDE

L ise should have seen the warning signs that all was not right as Adolph Hitler, Germany's new chancellor, rose to power in 1933. That same year the Jewish scientist, Einstein, renounced his German citizenship after accepting a position as a professor at Princeton University in America. Then Nazi followers in Berlin were encouraged to organize boycotts that ruined most Jewish businesses. The following year all Jewish scientists were forced out of their jobs in German universities. This included the elimination of Lise's own opportunities to lecture at the universities.

Lise and Otto were able to continue their research without interference from the government for the next few years, even when the Nuremberg Laws were passed in 1935, striping German Jews of their civil rights and forbidding them from marrying non-Jews. Most Germans continued to receive fair treatment under the laws, but the rights of Jews, other "undesirables," and people who opposed government policies became more and more restricted. Within a few years, people in these groups found that they could be jailed, relocated to fenced-in ghettos or lose their property with little or no defense.

Hitler's passionate speeches, conveying his dreams of a glorious, expanded nation of Germany, were enthusiastically embraced by cheering crowds of German citizens. However, Lise understood that people with Jewish ancestors had no place in his dreams, as he began to speak openly of his belief that Jews were an inferior race.

Hitler entered his new office with a hatred for Jewish people. Under his leadership, prejudice against women in science was replaced by a deadly prejudice against anyone with Jewish ancestors. He blindly blamed Jews for Germany losing the Great War (World War I), and the economic hardships Germany was enduring. He even believed Einstein and other Jewish scientists were contaminating pure science with their ideas. Hitler had also come to believe that Jews and certain other races were inferior, even subhuman, and must be eliminated to avoid intermarriages with Germans.

Unknown to Lise at the time, Hitler's plan was to eventually rid Germany of all remnants of Jewish people by any means possible. Having been baptized as a Protestant in 1908, Lise regarded herself as a Christian. But this meant nothing to the ruthless new leaders of Germany; nor did her service during World War I as an x-ray nurse for the Austrian armies, an ally of Germany. Only her ancestry mattered under Germany's cruel racial laws.

Inspired since boyhood by Charles Darwin's ideas about human evolution, Hitler believed that the Aryans had evolved from an old group of Europeans into a superior species, identified by their race. Hitler dreamed that German Aryans would one day form a ruling master race of superior people, while certain other races, made up of what he believed were inferior or subhuman people, would have to be contained or eliminated. His ideas were cemented by reading and absorbing the ideas from large numbers of books and articles written by both fanatical racists and respected scientists. What Lise didn't understand was how far Hitler was willing to go to make his dreams a reality.

He had already given much thought about how these ideas could be applied to the shaping of human cultures. Conversations with people who studied animal breeding convinced him that humans could be intentionally bred, much like cattle or horses, to improve the quality of the Aryan race.

During the early 1900s, some leading anthropologists from both America and Europe openly advocated a polygenetic evolution, by which they meant that each race had become a separate species through the process of evolution, with the Aryan race superior and certain other races inferior or subhuman. Even many scholarly articles and books supported the Nazi race laws and a belief that some races, such as Jews and Negroes, were probably below the level of beasts. Ernst Haeckel, a highly respected zoology professor, endorsed Hitler's policies and was a huge influence in convincing influential countrymen that Hitler was right in addressing this problem.

The support for these ideas provided by leading doctors and scientists gave Hitler's racist ideas great credibility and justified the Nazi racial laws. Polygenetics was a dangerous idea that supported the extreme racist belief that some races were not fully human. This was in direct opposition to biblical teachings that all humans belong to the same race, because everyone is a descendant of one original man and one original woman who were designed and created by God and made in His image.

Hitler saw the principles of Darwinian evolution and eugenics as the keys to a master race and thought it could and should be sped up by political means. The extreme forms of eugenics meant getting rid of the so-called inferior races, as well as handicapped individuals that might increase the inferior genes in the culture. At the same time, laws and policies promoted large families among members of the Aryan race. Hitler made Social Darwinism one of the foundations of his government. When he assumed power, his initial goals were to engineer a master race and get rid of the entire Jewish race.

By this time, Lise could no longer ignore the danger of living under Hitler's policies, but she still could not bring herself to make plans to leave Germany. Otto had often reassured Lise that because she was an Austrian citizen and worked for a private institution, she did not have anything to worry about.

Meanwhile, Hitler steadfastly pursued his plans for eliminating the world's Jews and other races he deemed worthless, intentionally causing their deaths by any means possible. Early in World War II, Nazi mobile killing units were sometimes ordered to kill groups of Jewish men, women, and children in mass shootings. Although they were told that Jews were no more than animals, such cruel actions were not good for troop morale. This forced Hitler to devise an alternative plan that involved sending Jews and other "undesirables" to work camps where the workers were forced to work long hours without adequate food or rest. They often died from exhaustion, starvation, or illness, while many more were killed in gas chambers. The enormous number of bodies were disposed of in crematoria. The camps were out of sight of most people, but nearby German citizens were suspicious that bad things were going on inside. At the same time, many people with mental or physical handicaps were taken to government hospitals where they often mysteriously died. Hitler hated the Christian teaching that weak and helpless people should be cared for. He eventually saw Christians who resisted his plans as enemies who stood in his way and needed to be eliminated themselves.

Lise had limited knowledge of the atrocities ordered by Hitler until after the War, when she found the courage in fiery speeches to condemning well-educated doctors and scientists for assisting Hitler in carrying out his evil plans.

The second stage in Hitler's plans to produce a master race involved providing plenty of living space in which they and their large families could flourish. In rapid succession, German armies annexed Austria and part of Czechoslovakia. In 1939 their armies invaded Poland. With that, World War II began.

In spite of the obvious signs, Lise had stubbornly held out hope that the situation in Germany would improve. After all, Germany had produced some of the most talented musicians, writers, scientists, theologians, philosophers, inventors, and thinkers in history, as well as some of the greatest institutions of higher learning and research. How could it be that a brilliant scientist as respected and well-known as Dr. Lise Meitner would soon be forced to flee for her life from the heart of Germany?

Review and Expand Your Knowledge

1. What was the human race that Hitler considered most inferior or subhuman? Did he consider the Negro race as "superior" or "inferior?" Compare Christian beliefs with Hitler's beliefs about human beings.

2. What group of people opposed Hitler because they believed that the first human parents were created by God in His image, so that all their descendants were fully human with no sub-human races or animal ancestors?

3. What did Charles Darwin propose about the evolution of all living things? In the story, what famous scientist supported Darwin's theory of evolution? Are there scientists today who support this theory? Are there scientists who do not support Darwin's theory?

4. German armies invaded what European country in 1939 after annexing Austria and parts of other German-speaking countries? This was the beginning of what war?

5. Name four famous Germans who were either a musician, writer, scientist, theologian, or philosopher.

CHAPTER 4

WATCHING THE
DREAM DISAPPEAR

D r. Lise Meitner glanced at her calendar in the dim morning light, noting the date, July 13, 1938. Life in Berlin, Germany had been the fulfillment of her dreams, but since the arrival of Hitler in 1933 as Germany's new Chancellor, they had turned into a nightmare. During the same time, most of the Jewish people living in Germany had seen their rights systematically taken away. Lise's love for her work blinded her to the obvious dangers she faced because of her Jewish heritage, but she was now forced to face reality.

Lise tried to calm her jumbled thoughts as she poured a steaming cup of coffee and dressed for work. She gathered the things she would

Hahn and Meitner in Emil Fischer's Chemistry Institute in Berlin, 1909.

need for the day, but the fact was, she had no idea what this day would bring.

Cracking open her front door, Lise glanced both ways before stepping out into the street. Because of her Jewish ancestry, she was now on a watch list. The Gestapo, Adolf Hitler's dreaded secret police, could be waiting for her around the next corner. Lise desperately hoped nothing appeared unusual as she walked to work at the prestigious Kaiser-Wilhelm Institute for Science in Berlin, Germany, on this ordinary Tuesday.

In only a few days, she would be forced to resign from the Institute because of her Jewish ancestry and be unable to find employment anywhere in Germany. As a scientist, she was not allowed to leave the country. An imminent arrest with relocation to a ghetto or a work camp loomed in her future. Lise had no alternatives. She had to get out. Only a few loyal friends knew about her plans to escape from Berlin.

For the past few weeks, a small group of friends had been frantically trying to put together a plan for Lise to escape from Germany and find employment elsewhere. Niels Bohr, a longtime friend and famous scientist himself, had finally negotiated with a scientific facility in Sweden to allow her to work there. Now, time was running out.

As soon as she arrived at work, Otto motioned her into his office where he informed her the plans had changed. Today would be her last day at the Institute. She would stay at work until 8:00 p.m., hurry back to her room, pack up a few essentials, and spend the night at the Hahn home. In the morning, she would leave by train for a "vacation" in Holland. As terrified as she was of being arrested, the finality of her work and her life in Berlin hit her like a brick missile. With her emotions teeter-tottering back and forth, she silently made her way to her work area. Even the familiar aroma of a hot cup of coffee did little to bring her comfort.

Throughout the day, Hahn tried to reassure Lise everything would be all right, but he was anything but convincing. His usual self-confident manner gone, he paced the floor and repeatedly wiped the sweat from his face. He had been advising Lise only months before that she had nothing to fear from Hitler because she worked in a private institute and was a citizen of Austria. That was no longer the case. After the annexation of Austria into the Third Reich in March of 1938, all Austrians immediately became subject to German laws, including the notorious Nazi racial laws. Lise could be arrested and sentenced with little hope for a fair trial.

Her presence also posed a danger for others. German authorities had already expressed their displeasure that one of the Institute's employees was Jewish. Having Lise as a research partner did not look good for Otto.

In spite of the increasing danger, Lise had been reluctant to leave. She'd overcome many barriers and worked hard to achieve her dream of becoming a scientist only to watch that dream die. Her leaving also meant she would lose her pension, the money in her bank account, and probably all of her possessions. In addition, Germany had been her home for the past thirty-one years, and she would miss it terribly. But remaining in Berlin would be even more disastrous for her. Resigned that her only option was to attempt an escape from Germany, she spent her last day at work focused on the task of correcting a paper written by a young associate.

As the hands on the clock approached 8:00 p.m., Lise accepted what had to be done. She picked up a few personal items and walked slowly to the door. Fear had driven her decisions for weeks. Now, as she closed the door for the last time to the work she loved, the only emotion she felt was anguish. It was all so unfair! How could the dream she had pursued so tenaciously be evaporating before her eyes?

But waiting from a variety of locations in Berlin were determined friends, focused on the urgency of what had to be done. They included Paul Rosbaud, the editor of a well-known German scientific journal; her friend, Dirk Costner; and two other longtime physicist friends. Everyone was afraid that Lise had waited too long to get out safely.

Otto nervously accompanied Lise to her apartment, giving up all efforts to be subtle as he tried to hurry her getaway. His career, as well as his life, could be in serious jeopardy if he were found in Lise's apartment helping a Jew escape from Germany. She packed only a few summer clothes and other essentials for her trip to Holland to keep up appearances that she was just going on a vacation and not leaving Germany permanently. Otto promised to ship her books, furniture, winter clothes, and other belongings later. She was hopeful that could happen, but right now, her possessions were the least of her worries.

Paul drove Lise and Otto to the Hahn home and explained the rest of the plan. He would pick Lise up in the morning and drive her to the train station where Dirk would be waiting. She was to act surprised at meeting him, and they would continue the trip together.

The plan seemed to be coming together. However, no one was aware that Kurt Hess, a fellow scientist at the Institute, had somehow learned about her plans to escape. A fanatical supporter of Hitler's visions, he had already sent a note to the Nazi authorities informing them of Lise's intentions to leave the country.

Review and Expand Your Knowledge

1. What happened in March of 1938 that made Lise subject to all the German racial laws?

2. Lise's friends knew she had no choice but to escape from Germany. What would probably have happened if she had not been able to escape?

3. Why did Lise not pack any winter clothes in her suitcase?

CHAPTER 5

THE ESCAPE

The next morning, Paul Rosbaud arrived to drive Lise to the train station. As a parting gift, Otto gave his longtime friend a diamond ring that had belonged to his mother. He said it could always be used as an emergency source of funds. As they neared the train station, Lise suddenly begged Paul to turn around and take her home. She couldn't face the prospect of leaving her dearest friends and the position at work she had achieved at such sacrifices. But, ultimately logic prevailed. She had to try to leave Germany because there was no other solution.

At the station, the Dutch physicist, Dirk Coster, greeted her with mock surprise and escorted her on board. Lise clutched her now outdated Austrian passport and said a nervous and grateful good-bye, knowing that several friends had put their lives and careers in danger to help her escape.

Many people had spent the past few days writing letters in coded language, arranging secret meetings, and cautiously making other arrangements. Niels Bohr had persuaded a friend to find Lise employment at the Nobel Institute of Theoretical Physics in Stockholm,

Sweden. Unknown to Lise at the time, a number of other scientists were also involved in trying to help her escape from Germany. It was about to be seen whether or not all their efforts would pay off.

As the train left Berlin, Lise felt a combination of sadness, relief, and anger. It was hard not to dwell on the unfairness of this day. She had spent years overcoming the prejudices many people had for women in the field of science to become one of the top scientists in Europe.

At the age of fifty-nine, she was in the prime of her scientific research skills with an impressive record of coauthoring over twenty published professional articles about the research she and Otto had been conducting. They were right in the middle of the most exciting research of her life, and she had been robbed of the opportunity to finish it. They were trying to repeat and make sense of nuclear research that was being conducted in Italy under Enrico Fermi and in France under Irene Curie-Joliot. The experiments involved bombarding uranium with "slowed" neutrons. They expected the atoms to change into another element slightly heavier or lighter than uranium in a process known as artificial transmutation, but none of the results indicated this was happening. This left Lise thinking they must have been mistaken about their results.

Lise and Otto were planning further tests involving the neutron bombardment of uranium when Lise was forced to leave Germany. The tantalizing unanswered questions had become a challenge Lise was looking forward to meeting. Throughout the long ride, her thoughts shifted back and forth between her fears and the uranium mystery. Finally, the train bumped and rattled, beginning the extended noisy process of slowing and coming to a stop. Safety and the Dutch border lay just ahead, but dozens of Nazi soldiers milled around the border crossing ready to arrest anyone who seemed suspicious. Lise and Dirk knew many people trying to leave Germany had been apprehended at the last moment and immediately sent to jail when their papers didn't appear legal.

The train had not yet come to a standstill when soldiers and Dutch border guards boarded. They walked deliberately through each car as if looking for someone and slowed their pace as they neared Lise. One of the guards stopped by her seat, towering over her. He took her passport without comment and continued walking toward the next car.

Fighting to hide her terror, Lise waited with as much poise as she could muster. She was the picture of a cultured lady, tastefully dressed in a simple dark-colored dress, her long hair pulled back neatly in a bun—not at all the image Hitler was striving to portray of a member of a supposed inferior race. The tension was almost unbearable as a full ten minutes passed. Dirk had spent days trying to work out an agreement with Dutch border officials to allow Lise to cross the border. Now, as Nazi soldiers roamed nearby, it appeared that his plan had failed.

Finally border guards reappeared in the doorway. Lise watched helplessly as they approached her. She struggled to keep her emotions in check, knowing that the next few seconds would reveal whether she would proceed to freedom or be arrested on the spot. One of the guards suddenly stopped beside her seat. Then he handed the passport back to her and quickly stepped off the train.

Lise and Dirk smiled weakly at each other. Lise was safe! At once, the train began to move. Two minutes later they crossed the border into Holland.

After brief visits with Dirk and his family in the Netherlands and Neils and his family in Copenhagen, she left for her new home in

Stockholm. She was grateful for a place of safety and employment, but she would face more challenges in a country where she was unable to speak the language and knew almost no one.

✡ ✠ ✡ ✠ ✡ ✠

Meanwhile in Berlin, the note informing authorities that Lise was planning to leave Germany mysteriously reappeared in the intelligence division. A person who secretly hoped Lise would be able to get away had intercepted the report, delaying the investigation. Now that Lise was safely over the border, the note resurfaced—too late to prevent her escape.

Review and Expand Your Knowledge

1. Research on radioactive elements were being conducted by three groups of Europeans in 1938. Who were the scientists and in what country did each of them live?
2. Of the countries that were conducting nuclear research, which ones fought with the Allies during World War II, and which fought against the Allies?
3. What would have happened to Lise if the German Nazi soldiers had realized Lise was permanently leaving Germany?
4. Describe the research on uranium Lise and Otto planned to repeat and study before Lise was forced to leave Germany.

CHAPTER 6

THE REVOLUTIONARY ATOMIC FISSION THEORY

During the Christmas holidays of 1938, Lise met her physicist nephew, Robert Frisch, in a small village in western Sweden for a week of vacation. Robert was the son of her sister, Gusti, and their relationship had always had a strong bond. Though she enjoyed time with her nephew, Lise's thoughts kept returning to a letter she'd received from Berlin.

Otto had kept Lise informed about the neutron bombardment experiments on uranium that continued at the Institute. In this latest letter, he wrote that one of the substances produced during their experiment seemed to be barium. But he didn't think it could be barium because that would indicate the uranium nucleus was breaking apart. Mainstream scientists at this time viewed the nucleus of an atom as a hard, solid structure that could be slightly altered, but breaking it into two large pieces was considered impossible. Nevertheless, Otto said a new chemical was being produced and it was behaving like barium. He wanted Lise's opinion about what might be happening.

Lise quickly engaged her nephew in a discussion about the mysterious results of the experiments as they went for a walk through a fresh layer of snow. Stimulated by the crisp winter air, their imaginations became freely creative. What if barium was forming as a result of the neutron bombardment of uranium? It was about half the size of a uranium nucleus. The presence of barium was certainly a clue that uranium nuclei might be splitting into two pieces.

Not only did most scientists believe the nucleus of an atom was a tightly packed mass of solid particles of mostly protons and neutrons, but they also knew that very strong forces were required to hold the nucleus together. But to break a nucleus into two nearly equal pieces? Impossible.

Doubting that current nuclear theory was completely correct, they began to search for another explanation. What if the uranium nucleus had properties of a liquid drop as Neils Bohr had once suggested? What if the absorption of an extra neutron caused such a nucleus to become wobbly, elongate, get thin in the middle, and separate into two positively charged pieces?

That much sounded logical, but they immediately saw a problem with this explanation. They knew that two positively charged objects would repel each other. Once the two new pieces began to separate, the large positive charges on each piece would cause them to forceful-ly fly apart from each other. The powerful forces that had been hold-ing the nucleus together would cause huge amounts of energy to be released in the process. None of the known ordinary sources of energy in an atom could account for this level of energy.

Lise first considered that uranium had ninety-two positive charges and barium had fifty-six. If uranium were breaking into two pieces, the other piece would have to be krypton, an odorless gas with thir-ty-six positive charges.

Lise persisted in the direction her logic was carrying her. Sitting on a snow-covered log and pulling complex formulas and measure-ments from her memory, she and Robert did calculations using scraps of paper and pencils found in their coats. They first calculated that the energy needed to drive the two pieces from the uranium nucleus apart was approximately 200,000,000 electron volts.

It was possible to account for such massive amounts of energy according to Einstein's $E = mc^2$ equation, but it would mean that a small amount of the uranium atom was actually disappearing and changing into energy.

They did more calculations to determine the mass of the original uranium atom and the mass of the new products. Their calculations indicated that a tiny amount of mass was completely disappearing from each uranium atom that split.

The final calculation was to apply Einstein's formula, $E = mc^2$, and determine the amount of energy that would be released. They quickly multiplied the missing mass times the speed of light times the speed of light again. The stunned scientists could only stare at their answer: roughly 200,000,000 electron volts. The amount of energy needed to split the uranium nucleus was the same as the amount of energy that would be released if a uranium atom split apart! Lise recognized that if this much energy were released by a large number of uranium atoms, the total energy would be unbelievably huge.

They now had a logical explanation for what was happening when uranium was bombarded with slowed neutrons. Uranium atoms were splitting in half, and in the process, small amounts of matter were disappearing and being converted into massive amounts of energy. This was just as Einstein had predicted many years ago. Being true scientists, they viewed their new ideas with considerable caution. Still, at this point, they were fairly confident they had found the correct explanation for what was happening during the uranium experiments.

Surrounded by the beauty of the snow-covered forest, Lise and Robert tried to take in the conclusion they had just reached. Although they did not yet know about the process of nuclear chain reactions, they expected that their new explanation would alter all of the current atomic theories. They understood that as soon as their ideas were published, scientists from all over the world would test and examine them in the most critical manner possible.

Meitner-Frisch Theory

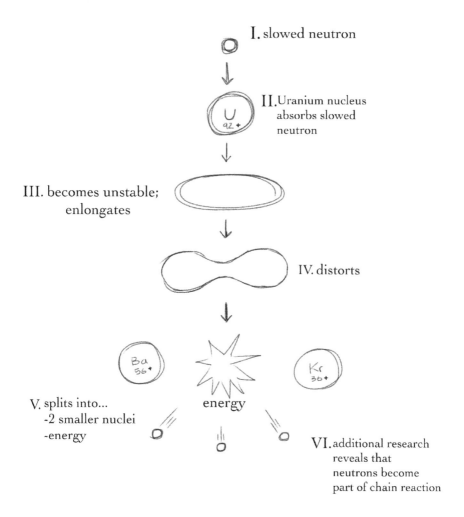

I. slowed neutron

II. Uranium nucleus
absorbs slowed
neutron

U
92 +

III. becomes unstable;
enlongates

IV. distorts

Ba
56 +

Kr
36 +

V. splits into...
-2 smaller nuclei
-energy

energy

VI. additional research
reveals that
neutrons become
part of chain reaction

But for now, the only two people in the entire world who had a valid explanation for the splitting of a uranium atom and the simultaneous release of nuclear energy were in a secluded forest in Sweden. They could not begin to imagine where this knowledge would lead the world in a few years.

Walking home, a decades-old incident from Berlin flashed in Lise's memory. Otto had once posted a sign on the door of their lab to scare away unwelcome government inspectors. The sign had read, "Warning. 200,000,000 volts." Lise laughed out loud as she thought about the old sign. The outrageous number had taken on a whole new meaning.

✡ ✠ ✡ ✠ ✡ ✠

At the same time in Berlin, Otto and his new assistant, Fritz Strassmann, confirmed the identity of barium as one of the new materials. Another element they identified was krypton. The uranium atoms were indeed breaking apart as they were bombarded with neutrons and producing new and smaller elements.

Review and Expand Your Knowledge

1. Who was Niels Bohr?
2. Who was Otto Robert Frisch?
3. What unexpected results were occurring in Dr. Hahn's experiments with uranium? Why did he ask Lise to try and explain what was happening?
4. Why did Lise and her nephew, Robert, first doubt that uranium atoms were breaking into two pieces?
5. How did Einstein's equation $E = mc^2$ solve the mystery of what was happening during the uranium experiments?
6. Write in words the meaning of $E = mc^2$.
7. Why was the presence of barium in the uranium experiments a clue that the uranium atoms were breaking into two parts?

CHAPTER 7

THE SWITCH: NUCLEAR ENERGY GOES TO AMERICA

Robert returned to work at the Copenhagen Institute in Denmark after visiting his Aunt Lise during Christmas vacation. He had only a few limited opportunities to talk with Neils Bohr, his boss and the director of the Institute, about the new atomic nuclear fission theory. He wanted his opinion about this before Bohr left for a science convention at Princeton, New Jersey. After briefly explaining the nuclear fission theory to him, Robert knew their logic was correct when Dr. Bohr slapped his forehead and exclaimed, "Oh, what idiots we have been!" Bohr strongly advised Robert and Lise to submit a paper about the new theory for publication as soon as possible.

As Dr. Bohr was leaving for America, Robert handed him two pages of a draft of the Meitner/Frisch article, which Dr. Bohr stuck in his pocket to read later. Promising to wait

Lecturing at Catholic University, Washington, D.C., 1946

until Lise and Robert had published their findings before releasing the news, he hurriedly left to begin his trip to America.

✡ ✠ ✡ ✠ ✡ ✠

Bohr felt certain that the Meitner/Frisch explanation was going to become one of the most significant scientific breakthroughs in many years. The long trip aboard the ship to America left many hours for him to analyze their explanation and eventually discuss it with Leon Rosenfeld, a fellow scientist also bound for the same science convention.

Then in a series of ironic twists, the center of nuclear research suddenly shifted from France, Germany, and Italy to the United States. It resulted from an incident that happened at the Princeton science convention.

Not understanding Dr. Bohr's promise to hold off on releasing the new theory, Dr. Rosenfeld joined a discussion group of physicists who were attending the convention. He shared with them all he had just learned about nuclear fission. The news was stunning! It created tremendous and instant excitement in the scientific community and set off a flurry of nuclear experiments and a rethinking of atomic theories. What Lise Meitner and Robert Frisch had discovered while sitting on a snow-covered log in the middle of a Swedish forest had suddenly been revealed to a roomful of top nuclear scientists in Princeton, New Jersey, USA.

A number of American scientists recognized there was a potential for a powerful new kind of nuclear weapon through atomic fission. At the same time, they were fearful that German scientists might have already begun work on such a weapon.

One of the scientists at the Princeton convention was Dr. Enrico Fermi from Italy. He had recently received a Nobel Prize for his research on atomic particles and had just arrived in the United States with his Jewish wife, Laura, and their two children.

When the first anti-Jewish laws were passed in Italy in September of 1938, he knew his family would be at risk before long. He then secretly accepted a position as a professor at Columbia University to begin as soon as he left Sweden. They made the decision to leave many of their possessions behind in Italy and travel directly from the Nobel Prize ceremonies in Sweden to the United States. This move put Fermi in place to use his knowledge to work on the problem of nuclear fission. Fermi himself was part of a team later on who determined that the fission of uranium atoms not only released massive amounts of energy, but additional neutrons were released that began a chain reaction.

Another key to placing nuclear research in America was a letter to President Franklin D. Roosevelt signed by the famous scientist, Albert Einstein, now a professor at Princeton University. The letter informed the president of new scientific discoveries which might lead to the development of a powerful nuclear bomb. The letter also advised that German scientists might already be working on such a weapon.

President Roosevelt somehow managed to secure funds to conduct a top-secret project to build the world's first controlled nuclear reactor. A team headed by Dr. Fermi was able to sustain and control the fission reactions of the uranium atoms.

This critical research provided the information that enabled scientists to build the world's first nuclear bomb in another top-secret project conducted in Los Alamos, New Mexico under the code name Manhattan Project. Some of the scientists present at the Princeton conference, along with other top Allied scientists, were recruited to do the work of building the bomb.

When Winston Churchill agreed to combine Britain's atomic research with the Manhattan Project, Lise's nephew, Robert Frisch, immediately moved to Los Alamos to work on the project. Lise was also given the opportunity to participate in the research, but knowing the kind of destruction a nuclear weapon might cause, she firmly turned down the offer. Memories of her time as a nurse in World War I with horribly wounded soldiers screaming in pain would not allow her to help build a weapon that had even the slightest potential to cause mass destruction and death.

Allied scientists and engineers worked furiously to complete the powerful bomb before the Germans. They were correct in suspecting that there was a highly secret military project in Berlin to develop a nuclear weapon for Germany. Begun in 1939, it was conducted by a group who called themselves the Uranium Club and included the famous scientist Werner Heisenberg and, Lise's former partner, Otto Hahn. But their efforts were years behind what the Allies had accomplished.

Then on July 16, 1945, seven years after Lise escaped from Berlin, the world's first atomic bomb was secretly exploded in a New Mexico desert to see what the powerful weapon would do. Its devastating effects shocked even the scientists who built it.

President Truman made the difficult decision to drop the remaining two atomic bombs on two Japanese military cities in an effort to end the war. Lise received the news that a nuclear bomb had been dropped on Hiroshima on August 6, 1945, with tears and shock. She always knew there was a possibility that nuclear energy could be channeled into a powerful weapon, but she had hoped the problems encountered in doing so would be insurmountable.

Review and Expand

1. Who was Dr. Enrico Fermi?
2. Why did Dr. Fermi accept a position as a professor at Columbia University and move his family directly to America after receiving a Nobel Prize?
3. What famous scientist signed a letter to President Roosevelt warning him that new scientific research in Germany might result in a powerful nuclear weapon and urged him to find a way to begin secret research on this in America?
4. What scientist headed a top-secret project in which the fission reactions of uranium atoms were sustained and controlled?
5. What was the Manhattan Project?
6. What two well-known scientists tried to develop a nuclear weapon for Germany?
7. What happened on July 16, 1945?
8. What difficult decision did President Truman make to end Japan's role in World War II?
9. Was Lise pleased that she and Robert had been able to explain the mystery of why barium was produced in the uranium experiments? Was she pleased that a nuclear bomb had been built on this discovery?

CHAPTER 8

REMEMBERING THE GOOD TIMES AND THE BAD TIMES

L ise was eighty-two when she moved to Cambridge to be near her nephew, Robert Frisch, and his wife and two children. They treated her as they would their own mother. She lived a peaceful life as she recalled how she had achieved her dream of becoming a scientist.

Knowing she had overcome seemingly insurmountable obstacles to complete her doctorate in physics, coauthor articles in prestigious scientific journals, and conduct cutting-edge research brought her satisfaction. As important as her work had been, her memories of life in Berlin also included the pleasant times spent with her fellow scientists.

Physicist Lise Meitner with students (Sue Jones Swisher, Rosalie Hoyt and Danna Pearson McDonough) on the steps of the chemistry building at Bryn Mawr College. Courtesy of Bryn Mawr College. (April 1959)

Inevitably, thoughts of the happiness in her life before Hitler rose to power were gradually pushed aside by memories of his misguided dreams of engineering a master race. The unfairness of the situation in July of 1938 was almost more than Lise could bear. In the end, a risky escape from Germany had been her only option.

But her biggest disappointment came when she learned that over the years, her research partners in Berlin had given her almost no credit for her role in the discovery of nuclear fission. Otto Hahn wrote numerous autobiographies and memoirs related to the fission discovery. He promoted the idea that the discovery was an achievement of German science and would have been made without physics and without Lise's input.

Otto downplayed Lise's role in their uranium nuclear research and referred to her occasionally as his assistant. Bragging on his involvement in discovering that barium appeared when uranium was bombarded with neutrons, he concluded that the presence of barium proved that uranium was breaking apart. A number of German scientists tried to rewrite the history of the discovery of nuclear fission and insisted that the Meitner- Frisch team had contributed nothing of value.

Another legend-type narrative evolved that said the brave German scientists had refused to build a nuclear bomb. However, that did not seem to be the case either. When the German nuclear scientists heard the news in 1945 that the Allies had dropped nuclear bombs on Japan, they had already been arrested. They were housed in a facility that was wired to record all their conversations to make sure they had not managed to build their own nuclear weapons. The hidden tapes revealed their great shock and surprise, along with injured pride that German scientists had not been able to accomplish the same thing first.

The extent to which Lise's contributions had been covered up became evident when the delayed Nobel Prize for Chemistry for 1944 was awarded only to Otto Hahn for his work on nuclear fission. The committee was reported to have engaged in a heated debate about who should receive the honor. When Otto was finally awarded the prize in 1946, he seemed to have no remorse over what the Germans had done during the war. Rather he focused on how much postwar Germany was suffering. Nor did he mention Dr. Lise Meitner during his acceptance speech as a valuable coworker. The team of Meitner-Hahn had been jointly nominated for the prize numerous times, and most of the credit for explaining nuclear fission belonged to Lise. Not being included with Hahn as an equal partner was a painful blow.

When offered her old job back at the Kaiser Wilhelm Institute in 1947 to work with Hahn and Strassmann, Lise turned it down. The friendship and trust between Lise and Otto had been damaged beyond repair.

Still, Lise's dreams did not die. After the war ended, she worked a few more years as a research scientist, but her final contribution to the field of science came as a speaker and lecturer. Until her health declined shortly before her death at age 89, she gave fascinating lectures about the history of nuclear energy. She also channeled her life lessons in two directions—to use knowledge about nuclear energy for peaceful endeavors and to encourage women to enter fields of science. Her normally shy nature gave way to indignation as she aimed powerful criticisms toward the German scientists and medical doctors who showed little remorse for their role in enabling Hitler to carry out his crimes against humanity.

Then, as if to make up for the years of unfair treatment, an overflow of honorary degrees, awards, and coveted prizes came from all over the world. Still shy and unassuming, Lise was a little embarrassed by all the public attention as numerous scientific and secular groups gave tribute to her as one of the world's greatest scientists. She nevertheless found fulfillment in looking back over her life and knowing she had been a pioneer of twentieth-century science. Perhaps her greatest sense of achievement came as she saw thousands of young women walk through doors to fields of science she had helped to open because she refused to let go of her dreams.

Review and Expand Your Knowledge

1. Who was the only scientist to receive the 1944 Nobel Prize for the discovery of nuclear fission?

2. The scientists who were on a team to build a nuclear weapon for Germany tried to explain that they bravely refused to complete a nuclear bomb for Hitler. What did hidden microphones in their quarters reveal to American intelligence officers about this?

THE SURROUNDING STORIES

Note: Reading the story of one woman's life provides great insight into the time period leading up to and following World War II. But the back stories give even more understanding and show how the events are connected. Students should read *Tenacious Dreams,* as well as the Surrounding Stories, and then answer the following questions and select projects to complete.

✡ ✠ ✡ ✠ ✡ ✠

Within months of his inauguration in 1933, Hitler pushed through legislation that dismissed all non-Aryan employees from government positions. Many top German universities lost more than a fourth of their scientific staff at this time. Almost a dozen scientists who lost their positions from this legislation were present or future Nobel laureates who accepted positions in American and European universities or research facilities. The Jewish scientist, Albert Einstein, whose theories about physics were severely criticized by Nazi supporters, had already become a professor at Princeton in New Jersey. Other top Jewish scientists made important contributions to U.S. scientific research in various fields.

✡ ✠ ✡ ✠ ✡ ✠

The 1936 Olympics were held in Berlin, Germany. Hitler expected this to be an opportunity to showcase his top Aryan athletes to the world. Several of the African Americans on the United States team were superb athletes, with Jesse Owens winning four gold medals in track and field. Hitler was furious that men from a so-called inferior race had defeated many of his best athletes. He exerted great pressure on Olympic directors to see that the two talented Jewish runners for the Americans did not compete. It was bad enough that Negro athletes had defeated his best runners, but being defeated by Jewish athletes would be even more humiliating.

✡ ✠ ✡ ✠ ✡ ✠

Dr. Max Planck is known as the father of quantum theory. A number of scientific institutions are named in his honor. He was one of the few scientists who was ever brave enough to criticize Hitler to his face over his treatment of Jewish scientists. Hitler responded by flying into a rage and doubling down on orders that Jewish scientists were not permitted to work in government institutions, nor allowed to leave the country.

Planck's personal life was marked with tragedies and hardships. After losing three of his five children as young adults, his son Edwin was accused of an assassination attempt on Hitler's life and executed. The final tragedy was the bombing of Dr. Planck's home during the last weeks of World War II.

✡ ✠ ✡ ✠ ✡ ✠

In 1940, German troops invaded and occupied Denmark. Dr. Neils Bohr received offers of employment from both the United States and Britain. He resolutely turned them down in order to help the Jewish people in Denmark and to help displaced scientists find a place to go. Two years later, the Gestapo decided to arrest the entire Jewish population and establish martial law. In the midst of these events, Dr.

Bohr received a message from a trusted source that an arrest warrant for him had already been issued from Berlin. It would likely be carried out within hours. Nazi leaders did not want to take a chance that Dr. Bohr would use his scientific knowledge to help the Allies.

With help from friends and only minutes to spare, arrangements were made for Dr. Bohr and his wife to escape. They crossed the Oresund Sound by night in a small boat to Sweden. The rest of his family, along with thousands of others, also made the risky trip to safety. Later, Dr. Bohr flew out of Sweden, crossing enemy territory to England. When the pilot flew at a higher elevation to evade detection, Dr. Bohr failed to put on his oxygen mask. He had already passed out and turned blue when a crew member discovered his condition. Nevertheless, the plane landed safely in Allied territory, and Dr. Bohr recovered from his close call. He later moved to New Mexico and became part of the Manhattan Project.

✡ ✠ ✡ ✠ ✡ ✠

Even though American fears of a German-made nuclear bomb were justified, the project never reached the level of a serious threat or got to the place of actually building an atomic bomb. While the American and British scientists were greatly motivated by fears that Germany already had a head start on building a nuclear weapon, Hitler and his German military leaders lacked a driving enthusiasm for the project. One of the reasons Germany did not push harder on their nuclear project was because Hitler was critical of the science of nuclear physics and thought it was contaminated by ideas of Jewish scientists. If not for Lise and her discoveries, the Germans might have eventually developed a powerful nuclear weapon, which would have been used against America and the other Allied forces. But time, location, and circumstances placed the discovery of nuclear fission in the hands of the Allies early on.

✡ ✠ ✡ ✠ ✡ ✠

As soon as the world's scientists learned about the fission of uranium nuclei, there was a rethinking of long-accepted atomic theories. By the end of February 1939, nuclear fission had been confirmed by dozens of scientists, although credit for Meitner and Frisch's role was often lost in the hectic efforts to test and retest ideas about nuclear fission. By March 1939, a scientific team in Paris and another team at Columbia reported that several free neutrons were released from each uranium that split. They immediately recognized that these free neutrons might start a chain reaction, which would be capable of generating huge quantities of energy. One of these scientists was Enrico Fermi, who was later selected to head the critical research demonstrating that nuclear reactions in uranium could be contained and controlled.

✡ ✠ ✡ ✠ ✡ ✠

Another weapon Hitler did not favor early in the war was rockets, but during the final months of the war they were used extensively to bomb England. Bombs were attached to the V-2 rockets their scientists had developed. They were delivered over long distances, causing great destruction where they landed. Just days before the War ended, the top German rocket scientist, Wernher von Braun, and many of his coworkers, were receiving mixed messages about their fate. There was a possibility they would be shot to keep them from going to an enemy camp. There was also a possibility that they would be captured by Russian soldiers and sent to Russia. They did not want to be taken prisoners by anyone except American troops. They eventually decided to send von Braun's younger brother out on a bicycle and instructed him to look for an American soldier. His job was to tell an American military unit that a group of German rocket engineers wanted to surrender to them. The young von Braun spent considerable time trying to convey this message in broken English to the first American soldier he found. But eventually a young boy on a bicycle was able to convince an American military unit that the top German rocket engineer and his coworkers wanted to surrender to them. Von Braun later moved to the United States and joined a U.S. rocket research group. He became head of NASA's Marshall Space Flight Center that designed the Saturn V rockets used to put a man on the moon. Many German rocket scientists and technicians moved to the United States and worked in the space program. Others went to Russia and helped develop the first Sputnik satellite, which was put into space by German-designed rockets.

✡ ✠ ✡ ✠ ✡ ✠

World War II finally came to an end in 1945 when Allied military forces defeated German and Italian armies and nuclear bombs were detonated on two key Japanese military cities, forcing Japan to surrender. Historians estimate that 50,000,000 people lost their lives as a result of the war.

✡ ✠ ✡ ✠ ✡ ✠

Six million Jews who were unable to escape the Nazi government died under Hitler's orders. Many Jewish men, women, and children were sent to concentration camps, where they were treated with great brutality. As the War ended, the whole world looked in horror at the inhumane treatment of the people who were forced to live there. This time of persecution of the Jews has come to be known as the Holocaust. Lise thought back to the terrifying day she left Berlin. She realized that a work camp would have been her destiny had friends not made a way for her to escape.

✿ ✠ ✿ ✠ ✿ ✠

Nazi officials also ordered the murders of millions of other people, including European Christians, Gypsies, Slavic Russians, Poles, Mongolians, and European black Africans. When Hitler realized that Germany had been defeated by the Allies, he committed suicide. The Nuremburg Trials brought prison or death sentences to most of the other top Nazi leaders.

✿ ✠ ✿ ✠ ✿ ✠

After many of the Jewish survivors realized they had no home or family to return to after the War, they chose to immigrate to the ancient land of their forefathers known as Palestine. In 1947 a United Nations resolution recommended that a small portion of Palestine be recognized as the independent nation of Israel. On May 14, 1948, Israel declared itself to be an independent nation.

✿ ✠ ✿ ✠ ✿ ✠

Not long after World War II ended, Russia also produced and tested nuclear weapons. Some of the people working within America's nuclear weapons projects sent classified, secret information about the building of nuclear weapons to Russia. During the war, Russia and the U.S. were allies, but within a few years, Communist Russia and the United States became dangerous enemies. Both countries built huge supplies of nuclear weapons. Several other countries now possess nuclear bombs in spite of international efforts to stop the spread of nuclear weapons. The international community is trying to restrain the spread of more nuclear weapons.

✡ ✠ ✡ ✠ ✡ ✠

Hitler remained convinced that the world would someday thank him for eliminating what he considered the parasitic Jews and other inferior races in order to rebuild the superior Aryan species. Instead, Hitler is remembered today as one of the world's most evil men for ruining the lives or causing the deaths of millions of people. Like the evil Haman in Esther's day, his life ended in perpetual disgrace.

✡ ✠ ✡ ✠ ✡ ✠

The international science community continued to recognize Dr. Lise Meitner's contributions to science even after her death. In 1992, as a permanent memorial to her genius, element 109 on the Periodic Table was assigned the name Meitnerium.

Review and Expand Your Knowledge
I. Discuss, write or complete the following assessments of what you have learned.

1. Of the following countries, which ones fought with the Allies during World War II? Which ones fought against the Allies? England, France, Germany, Italy, Japan, Russia, U.S.

2. Write a few sentences about why Hitler dismissed all Jewish professors from German universities and tell how this was a great benefit to American universities and research centers.

3. Write a few sentences about Adolph Hitler's motivation to

expand Germany and get rid of certain races. Where did Hitler get his ideas about promoting a master race and getting rid of what he considered inferior races?

4.   Write a few sentences about what Adolph Hitler did to get rid of the races he considered inferior.

5.   Write a few sentences about Lise Meitner's motivation for wanting to understand what happened when uranium was bombarded with slowed neutrons. Do you think she wanted her discovery to be used to build a nuclear weapon? Tell how the field of science is different from the field of technology.

6.   In 1938, the world's major centers for nuclear research were in France, Italy and Germany. Write a few sentences about how the United States became the world's major center for nuclear research a few years later.

7.   How did Russia get top secret instructions on how to build a nuclear bomb?

8.   Lise Meitner is often referred to as a pioneer for women scientists. What does this mean? Why were women pioneers in science important?

9.   In your own opinion, tell why you think only Otto Hahn received the Nobel Prize for the discovery of nuclear fission and Lise Meitner was not included.

10.   Write a few sentences about why Wernher von Braun and his associates sought out American troops to whom they could surrender after the War. Tell how they were able to find American troops.

11.   How did Jesse Owens and Lise Meitner demonstrate that Hitler's master race belief was wrong?

12.   How did Hitler use propaganda to influence people to dislike

Jews and certain other races? Is propaganda used today to influence how people think about certain politicians and groups? Try to give an example.

13. What is the difference between believing all humans were developed by a polygenetic route and believing humans are all descendants of the first man and woman designed and created by God?

14. Germany, Italy, and Japan made up the Axis Powers during World War II. Each country was under the leadership of a dictator who had acquired the authority to make decisions for the country. The United States, the United Kingdom, and France had presidents, but these men did not have complete authority over these countries. Leadership was shared with other groups. When the United States was first established as a republic in 1776, the founders made sure there were three co-equal branches of government rather than one king who ruled over the nation. What are the advantages of the American form of government?

15. The terms "white supremacy" and "eugenics" are renounced throughout the nation. What does each term means? How are they similar to the things Hitler believed?

II. Choose a creative way to report on one of the people mentioned in the book.

Here are several suggestions.

1. Use a large poster sheet, cut out an opening for their face, and draw hair, a hat, and other characteristic features around the face. Alternatively, other kinds of props may be used. Speak in first person, such as, "I left a mark on history, because . .

.", pretending to be the person you chose. Tell something about the person's life. You may also speak as someone who knew a lot about this person, such as, "I first met __. . ."

2. Write a letter from your character to one of his/her friends. The letter should talk about something significant in their life.
3. Write a radio interview with the character they chose. Use someone to be the character and someone to be the interviewer.
4. Write a news article or news report about the character.
5. Incorporate other methods, such as a rap, a song, a drama, etc., if your teacher approves.

III. Make a large timeline going from 1900 to 1945.

1. Show 1938 and write beside it "Lise Meitner escaped from Germany." Show 1939 when World War II began and 1945 when the war ended. Add other important dates mentioned in the story. Now try to get some personal information about your family and others you know. See if any of them joined the U.S. military during World War II. Did anyone immigrate to the U.S. from another country? Include birth and marriage dates of grandparents and great grandparents and other older relatives. Parents will need to help you find some of this information. Compare things that were going on in the U.S. at the same time other events were taking place in Europe and other places.

PARTIAL LIST OF REFERENCES

Jerry Bergman. *Hitler and the Nazi Darwinian Worldview.* Kitchener, Ontario, Canada: Joshua Press Inc. 2012.

Deborah Crawford. *Lise Meitner, Atomic Pioneer.* New York: Crown Publishers, Inc. 1969.

Laura Fermi. *Atoms in the Family: My Life with Erico Fermi.* Chicago & London: The University of Chicago Press. 1954.

Janet Hamilton. *Lise Meitner. Pioneer of Nuclear Fission.* Berkeley Heights, NJ: Enslow Publishers, Inc. 2002.

Ruth Lewin Sime. *Lise Meitner: A Life in Physics.* Berkley and Los Angeles: University of California Press. 1996.

ANSWERS TO CHAPTER QUESTIONS

CHAPTER 1

1. How were men and women treated differently during most of the nineteenth century in Austria when it came to opportunities to attend universities and acquire jobs? Were these problems also found in America?

Ans. During the early and mid-nineteenth century, Austrian public schools ended for girls after the age of 14. Except to prepare to be a teacher and improve in the subject they taught, women were excluded from attending rigorous high schools and universities with young men by law. Opportunities for young women began to change just before the beginning of the twentieth century. Advanced education became an option, although science and math courses continued to be filled mostly by young men.

Ans. Both boys and girls were given opportunities to attend school in America. The only prohibitions about attending certain schools were for black and Indian children.

2. Traditionally, what were young women in Austria expected to do within a few years after finishing public school?

Ans. Throughout most of the 1800s, young ladies were expected to prepare to marry and manage a home after completing about eight years of school.

CHAPTER 2

1. Find the meaning of these terms: *prejudice, bias, discrimination, propaganda, and racism.* Tell how Lise Meitner was affected by these problems.

Ans. Terms defined by Webster's Dictionary or Google definitions:

Prejudice – a biased opinion based on emotion rather than reason.

Bias – same as prejudice.

Discrimination – To distinguish or discriminate between someone or something on the basis of race, sex, class, or religion.

Propaganda – information, especially of a biased or misleading nature, used to promote or publicize a particular political cause or point of view.

Racism - the belief that different races possess distinct characteristics, abilities, or qualities, especially so as to distinguish them as inferior or superior to one another.

Ans. As a girl attending public school, Lise did not have the same educational opportunities as the boys. Females were discouraged from participating in many kinds of classes and careers, especially those heavy in mathematics and physics. Her pay scale for her first jobs was nowhere the same as what men were paid for doing the same job. As a person with Jewish ancestors, she experienced these same kind of biases, only more intensely.

2.   During the time when Lise was attending universities and finding her first job, were young women encouraged to pre-pare for or begin a career in science? Is that still true today?

Ans. *For the most part, Lise and other young women were not en-couraged to earn degrees in science or to enter careers in sci-ence. In fact, they tended to be discouraged to aim for scien-tific jobs. Lise had to overcome many biased traditions and opinions in order to earn her Ph.D. in physics, even though she was fully qualified to do the work.*

Ans. *The attitude toward women getting a science-related degree or working in a scientific field has completely changed since Lise was obtaining a Ph.D. degree and beginning a career in sci-ence. In today's culture, men and women obtain degrees and jobs primarily on their abilities rather than on their gender.*

3.   What unfair working conditions did Lise agree to when she first began conducting research in Berlin, Germany?

Ans. *For the first few years she worked as a nuclear researcher, she did not receive a salary or have a title. She was not allowed to enter the chemistry labs where men worked, and she had to work in a small basement room.*

4.   How did Lise overcome the misgivings her male coworkers had for a woman scientist?

Ans. *Lise gradually overcame the misgivings her male coworkers had for a female scientist by demonstrating her exceptional abilities, intelligence, and talent.*

5. Name several well-known people who were contemporaries of Lise (who lived from 1878 to 1968).

Ans. Einstein; Presidents Roosevelt, Truman, and Eisenhower; Anne Frank; Hitler; Jesse Owens; Wernher von Braun; Marilyn Monroe; many others.

6. Who was Dr. Otto Hahn?

Ans. Dr. Hahn was a German scientist who conducted nuclear research with Lise.

7. Who was Dr. Max Planck?

Ans. Dr. Planck was a famous German scientist who is known as the originator of the quantum theory, which greatly expanded our understanding of atomic and subatomic processes.

CHAPTER 3

1. What was the human race that Hitler considered most inferior or subhuman? Did he consider the Negro race as "superior" or "inferior"? Compare Christian beliefs with Hitler's beliefs about human beings.

Ans. The Jewish race.

Ans. Hitler also considered the Negro race as "inferior."

Ans. Most Christians believe God planned, designed and created the first man and woman in His image, and all humans descended from these original parents. Hitler embraced Darwin's ideas of evolution and believed human ancestors were ape-like animals who evolved into humans through random, unguided natural processes.

2.   What group of people opposed Hitler because they believed that the first human parents were created by God, so that all their descendants were fully human with no sub-human races or animal ancestors?

Ans.   Many Protestants and Catholics believed that God created the first human parents and rejected the idea that some people belonged to sub-human races.

3.   What did Charles Darwin propose about the evolution of all living things? In the story, what famous scientist supported Darwin's theory of evolution? Are there scientists today who support this theory? Are there scientists who do not support Darwin's theory?

Ans.   Darwin proposed that all living things—plants, animals, microbes, and humans—evolved from the first living organism, known as the Common Ancestor. The first living organism was proposed to have come into existence as just the right chemicals and conditions merged in a warm pond. Then this organism reproduced and formed other organisms that continued to reproduce until complex forms of life evolved through random unguided natural processes.

Ans.   Darwin's theory was supported by the scientist Ernst Haeckel.

Ans.   Most mainstream scientists support Darwin's theory today.

Ans.   More than eight hundred Ph.D. scientists are skeptical of claims from Darwin's theory of evolution that random mutation and natural selection account for the complexity of life and have signed a public document known as a "Scientific Dissent From Darwinism."

4. German armies invaded what European country in 1939 after annexing Austria and parts of other German-speaking countries? This was the beginning of what war?

Ans. Poland

Ans. World War II

5. Name four famous Germans who were either a musician, writer, scientist, theologian, or philosopher.

Ans. A few examples of famous Germans are the musicians and composers Bach, Beethoven, Brahms, Handel, and Mozart; Immanuel Kant; astronomers Copernicius and Kepler; Gutenburg; Martin Luther and Albert Schweitzer.

CHAPTER 4

1. What happened in March of 1938 that made Lise subject to all the German racial laws?

Ans. Austria was annexed by Germany, making all Austrian citizens subject to existing German laws, including the racial laws.

2. Lise's friends knew she had no choice but to escape from Germany. What would probably have happened if she had not been able to escape?

Ans. She would have been forced to resign from the Institute and be unable to find employment anywhere in Germany. As a scientist, she would not be allowed to leave the country. An imminent arrest with relocation to a ghetto or a work camp was likely.

3. Why did Lise not pack any winter clothes in her suitcase?

Ans. She was afraid it would look like she did not intend to return to Germany.

CHAPTER 5

1. Research on radioactive elements were being conducted by three groups of Europeans in 1938. Who were the scientists and in what country did each of them live?

Ans. Enrico Fermi in Italy, Irene Curie Joliot in France, and Lise Meitner and Otto Hahn in Germany.

2. Of the countries that were conducting nuclear research, which ones fought with the Allies during World War II, and which fought against the Allies?

Ans. France fought with the Allies and Germany and Italy fought against the Allies.

3. What would have happened to Lise if the German Nazi soldiers had realized Lise was permanently leaving Germany?

Ans. She would have been immediately arrested and sent to jail.

4. Describe the research on uranium Lise and Otto planned to repeat and study before Lise was forced to leave Germany.

Ans. They planned to repeat tests in which uranium was bombarded with slowed neutrons. They planned to do tests to identify any new elements that appeared and then to provide a scientific explanation for these results.

CHAPTER 6

1. Who was Niels Bohr?

Ans. *Born in Denmark, he established the Bohr Institute for Theoretical Physics in Copenhagen. Bohr's atomic model of a hydrogen atom showed that electrons travel in distinct orbits around the nucleus according to its quantum number. He was awarded the Nobel Prize for applying his atomic model to the elements on the Periodic Chart.*

2. Who was Otto Robert Frisch?

Ans. *He was Lise's nephew, the son of her sister, Gusti. He was a co-discoverer with Lise of the fission of uranium nuclei.*

3. What unexpected results were occurring in Dr. Hahn's experiments with uranium? Why did he ask Lise to try and explain what was happening?

Ans. *They expected new elements to form that were slightly heavier or slightly lighter than uranium. In their first tests, there was no sign of the expected new elements. Instead, one of the new elements seemed to be barium. Dr. Hahn did not think it was possible for barium to be forming in this experiment, but he thought Lise might find a good explanation for what was happening.*

4. Why did Lise and her nephew, Robert, first doubt that uranium atoms were breaking into two pieces?

Ans. *If uranium were breaking apart, it would mean all the current nuclear theories were wrong. According to current theories, nuclei were thought to be made up of neutrons and protons held together by extremely strong forces so that nuclear particles could only be used to chip off small pieces or add small pieces to them. It would take a tremendous amount of energy to cause a nucleus to break into two pieces, and there was no explanation for where there was enough energy to cause this.*

5. How did Einstein's equation $E = mc^2$ solve the mystery of what was happening during the uranium experiments?

Ans. *A huge amount of energy was released when a small amount of matter in the nucleus disappeared and changed into energy.*

6. Write in words the meaning of $E = mc^2$.

Ans. *Energy is equal to mass times the speed of light times the speed of light.*

7. Why was the presence of barium in the uranium experiments a clue that the uranium atoms were breaking into two parts?

Ans. *A barium atom had about half as much mass as a uranium atom. There weren't many other explanations for where barium could have come from other than for uranium to break apart.*

CHAPTER 7

1. Who was Dr. Enrico Fermi?

Ans. *He was an Italian scientist. He was awarded a Nobel Prize for his research about bombarding uranium with neutrons.*

2. Why did Dr. Fermi accept a position as a professor at Columbia University and move his family directly to America after receiving a Nobel Prize?

Ans. He left the Nobel Prize ceremonies in Sweden with his Jewish wife and children to accept a position in America after the first anti-Jewish racial laws were passed in Italy.

3. What famous scientist signed a letter to President Roosevelt warning him that new scientific research in Germany might result in a powerful nuclear weapon and urged him to find a way to begin secret research on this in America?

Ans. Albert Einstein

4. What scientist headed a top-secret project in which the fission reactions of uranium atoms were sustained and controlled?

Ans. Enrico Fermi

5. What was the Manhattan Project?

Ans. It was a top-secret research project to build a powerful weapon that released huge amounts of energy when uranium atoms split. The scientists working on this project thought the Germans were also trying to build a similar weapon and they were motivated to achieve this before the Germans did.

6. What two well-known scientists tried to develop a nuclear weapon for Germany?

Ans. Otto Hahn and Werner Heisenberg

7. What happened on July 16, 1945?

Ans. One of the nuclear bombs was exploded in order to measure and observe its destructive power.

8. What difficult decision did President Truman make to end Japan's role in World War II?

Ans. Nuclear bombs were exploded on two military cities in Japan to bring World War II to an end.

9. Was Lise pleased that she and Robert had been able to explain the mystery of why barium was produced in the uranium experiments? Was she pleased that a nuclear bomb had been built on this discovery?

Ans. She was pleased that she had been able to propose a logical theory for why barium was produced in the uranium experiments. She was not pleased that a nuclear bomb had been built on this discovery.

CHAPTER 8

1. Who was the only scientist to receive the 1944 Nobel Prize for the discovery of nuclear fission?

Ans. Otto Hahn

2. The scientists who were on a team to build a nuclear weapon for Germany tried to explain that they bravely refused to complete a nuclear bomb for Hitler. What did hidden microphones in their quarters reveal to American intelligence officers about this?

Ans. The microphones revealed that it was untrue that they chose not to build a nuclear weapon. They wanted an excuse for why American and Allied scientists were able to do this first.

THE SURROUNDING STORIES

I. Discuss, write or complete the following assessments of what you have learned.

1. Of the following countries, which ones fought with the Allies during World War II? Which ones fought against the Allies? England, France, Germany, Italy, Japan, Russia, U.S.

Ans. Fought with Allies: England, France, Russia, U.S.

Ans. Fought against Allies: Germany, Italy, Japan

2. Write a few sentences about why Hitler dismissed all Jewish professors from German universities and tell how this was a great benefit to American universities and research centers.

Ans. Hitler believed all Jews were inferior and were contaminating German citizens and institutions. His plan was to eliminate all Jews from Germany and eventually from the earth.

Ans. Many Jewish professors, especially scientists, were experts in their fields. They joined universities and research centers in other countries and helped their programs grow and improve.

3. Write a few sentences about where Adolf Hitler got his ideas to produce a master race?

Ans. He studied methods used by cattle breeders, as well as the accepted principles of how Darwinian evolution occurs. He concluded that by following these methods, humans could be made to evolve into a master race of people with great intelligence and athletic abilities.

4. Write a few sentences about why Adolph Hitler wanted to get rid of the races he considered inferior. How did he plan to do this?

64

Ans. He was afraid people from the "superior" races would marry people from the "inferior" races and contaminate the traits their children inherited.

Ans. He planned to start with the Jews and eliminate other "inferior" races later. At first Jewish men, women, and children were lined up and shot, but this was not good for troop morale. He then devised a plan to send them to work camps where many died from harsh treatment and others died in gas chambers. The dead bodies were cremated in ovens.

5. Write a few sentences about Lise Meitner's motivation for wanting to understand what happened when uranium was bombarded with slowed neutrons. Do you think she wanted her discovery to be used to build a nuclear weapon? Tell how the field of science is different from the field of technology.

Ans. As a scientist Lise wanted to discover and explain what was happening during her experiments.

Ans. She definitely did not want her discovery of nuclear fission to be used to build a nuclear weapon.

Ans. The field of science seeks to find explanations of observations or experiments about how, why, when, where, or under what conditions these things happen. The field of technology is sometimes called "applied science." It seeks to invent or build things, often based on scientific knowledge, that make work easier, faster, cheaper, or to fulfill a specific goal. Science looks for knowledge without being concerned about if it will be used for good things or bad things. Technology must make decisions about whether its inventions will be used in helpful ways or harmful ways. Sometimes technology inventions are both helpful and harmful.

6. In 1938, the world's major centers for nuclear research were in France, Italy and Germany. Write a few sentences about how the United States became the world's major center for nuclear research a few years later.

Ans. *Lise and her nephew were familiar with the uranium research going on in France, Germany, and Italy. They proposed a likely explanation for why barium seemed to be appearing in the German experiments as uranium was bombarded by slowed neutrons. They proposed that the uranium nuclei were breaking apart, forming two new elements and releasing huge amounts of energy. Robert wanted his boss, Neils Bohr, to give him his opinion about their discovery before he left for a science convention in America. Bohr immediately saw that their explanation explained the results perfectly and discussed this for hours with Leon Rosenfeld, a fellow scientist on the long boat trip to a science convention in New Jersey. Not understanding the need to wait until a Meitner-Frisch paper was in print, Rosenfeld shared what he had learned about nuclear fission and the release of huge amounts of energy with other Allied scientists. Soon top-secret research was underway in America to try and produce a nuclear weapon before German scientists did.*

7. How did Russia get top secret instructions on how to build a nuclear bomb?

Ans. *One or more scientists in the Manhattan Project sent classified information about the bomb to Russia, who was at this time fighting with the Allies.*

8. Lise Meitner is often referred to as a pioneer for women scientists. Why was this important?

Ans. *Lise was one of a few elite women scientists in the world who was conducting research about nuclear reactions. She had overcome the prejudice many people had against women scientists by her incredible intellectual abilities. As one of the first women to enter this field, she opened the door for other women to follow.*

9. In your own opinion, tell why you think only Otto Hahn received the Nobel Prize for the discovery of nuclear fission and Lise Meitner was not included.

Ans. *The answer to this may never be known. One possible reason may be because there was still bias and discrimination against women scientists. Another reason may be that Otto Hahn wrote several accounts about his role in this important scientific discovery that did not give credit to Lise for her role in discovering nuclear fission.*

10. Write a few sentences about why Wernher von Braun and his associates sought out American troops to whom they could surrender after the War. Tell how they were able to find American troops.

Ans. *They expected to be safe with American troops and did not want to be forced to go to Russia. They wanted to surrender to American troops and go to America with their expertise as rocket scientists. Dr. von Braun's younger brother rode a bicycle until he found an American soldier and convinced his outfit that the top rocket scientists in Germany were ready to surrender to the Americans.*

11. How did Jesse Owens and Lise Meitner demonstrate that Hitler's master race belief was wrong?

Ans. The African American runner, Jesse Owens, was a superior athlete who defeated Hitler's best athletes. Lise Meitner, who came from a long line of Jewish ancestors, was widely recognized as one of the world's top scientists. She made an important scientific discovery about nuclear fission that German scientists had not been able to discover first.

12. How did Hitler use propaganda to influence people to dislike Jews and certain other races? Is propaganda used today to influence how people think about certain politicians and groups? Try to give an example.

Ans. He continually released any kind of information he could, true or not, to discredit Jewish people. He did not allow Jews to be publicly honored in any way, even at funerals. So, everything most Germans heard about Jews was negative and nothing was positive.

Ans. Rival political groups sometimes do this same thing. Their political comments always portray their candidates and programs in very positive ways while political opponents and programs are always portrayed in the worst possible ways.

13. What is the difference between believing all humans were developed by a polygenetic route and believing humans are all descendants of the first man and woman designed and created by God?

Ans. *According to polygenetic human evolution, ape-like animals evolved into the different races by means of random, un-planned, unguided natural processes resulting in a few su-perior races and several inferior races. Believing that God planned, designed, and created the first man and woman in His image, who were the ancestors of all humans, shows that all humans have purpose and value and are not an accident. One of the foundations of our basic worldview beliefs is built on how we answer the question, "Where did I come from?"*

14. Germany, Italy, and Japan made up the main Axis Powers during World War II. Each country was under the leadership of a dictator who had acquired the authority to make deci-sions for the country. The main Allied forces, the United States, England, and France had presidents, but these men did not have complete authority over these countries. Leadership was shared with other groups. When the United States was first established as a republic in 1776, the founders made sure there were three co-equal branches of government rather than one king who ruled over the nation. What are the advantages of the American form of government?

Ans. *When kings have no one with authority over them, they are free to do anything they choose. Occasionally there are good decent kings, but most of the time, almost any king with unre-strained power will be tempted to do things that benefit them-selves and their friends rather than do what is best for the whole country. The American founders were determined not to give unlimited power to the leaders of their new country. They divided the governing leadership for America equally among the three branches of government—executive, judicial, and legislative. If the executive president is proceeding in an unwise direction, the other branches of government have the authority to prevent or alter what is happening.*

15. "White supremacy"and eugenics are renounced throughout America today. What do these terms means? How are they similar to the things Hitler believed and promoted?

Ans. "White supremacy" is a racist belief that members of the white race are smarter and better able to govern than are members of black or colored races. This belief led to policies that gave white citizens more rights and more leadership roles than blacks and colored citizens. At one time white supremacy was a widespread belief in America, but after the passage of civil rights legislation, it is only found in small pockets of the country today. These beliefs are very similar to Hitler's evolutionary beliefs about Jews, Negroes, and some other races. He believed the Aryan (white) race was more intelligent and more capable of governing than Jews, Negroes, and certain other races. Racial laws were passed in Germany to control the freedoms of the "inferior" race, restricting many personal choices, and not allowing them to have the same basic rights as the so-called "superior" races.

Ans. Eugenics refers to a belief that human populations can be improved by preventing people with undesirable traits from having children and encouraging people with desirable traits to have large families.

Hitler's beliefs were much more extreme, but they were similar to white supremacy and eugenics. He promoted laws that regulated who could and could not marry and have children, as well as allowing practices such as forced sterilization of so-called inferior races or the outright killings of members of some races to prevent them from "contaminating" the gene pool of the so-called superior races.

ACKNOWLEDGMENTS

As with any book, many people were part of this project. I would like to name a few:

- Tracy Crump for patiently advising and editing this story
- Charli Kendricks for her talented drawings
- Faithe Thomas for steering me through numerous requirements, recommendations and optional decisions